HEART DISEASE

CAROLINE ARNOLD

HEART DISEASE

Franklin Watts
New York / London / Toronto / Sydney / 1990
A Venture Book

Diagrams by Ruth Adam

Photographs courtesy of: Photo Researchers: pp. 20 (Frances Leroy, Biocosmos, Science Photo Library), 23 (Bettye Lane), 33 (Morris Huberland), 38 (Science Photo Library), 45 (Steve Skloot), 62, 77 (Gerry Cranham), 85, 93 (Bruce Roberts), 95; Phototake, NYC: p. 50 (David Wagner); AP/Wide World: p. 80; National Heart, Lung, and Blood Institute: pp. 87, 88.

Library of Congress Cataloging-in-Publication Data

Arnold, Caroline.
Heart disease / Caroline Arnold.
p. cm.—(A Venture book)
Includes bibliographical references.
Summary: Describes the heart and circulatory system and both genetic and acquired diseases that can adversely affect their functioning.
ISBN 0-531-10884-8
1. Heart—Diseases—Juvenile literature. [1. Heart—Diseases.
2. Circulatory system—Diseases.] I. Title.
RC681.A69 1990
616.1'2—dc20 90-33609 CIP AC

CONTENTS

*I dedicate this book to the
memory of Louis Glenn Zirkle,
Professor of Art, Grinnell
College, Grinnell, Iowa,
who taught me the value of
craftsmanship in all things.*

INTRODUCTION

It used to be that when a person's heart stopped beating, he or she was pronounced dead. The heart was the irreplaceable center of existence, and without it there was no life. Today, even though numerous techniques are available to maintain life after a person's own heart fails, the heart remains the most essential organ of the human body except for the brain. Day after day it maintains its steady rhythm, pumping blood through the rest of the body. Most of us can expect our hearts to keep us going well into our seventies or more, a remarkable feat considering the heart's constant use.

For some people, however, their hearts are not so reliable. Although we tend to think of heart disease as a problem of the elderly, that is not necessarily the case. More than 20 percent of those who die of heart attacks are under the age of sixty-five, and for many, signs of trouble begin much earlier.

Recent estimates predict that this year more than 1.5 million Americans will have heart attacks, and more than 540,000 will die from them. If you add to that number the people who die from blood vessel and other circulatory disorders, the number reaches nearly 1 million. This almost equals the combined deaths from cancer, accidents, pneumonia, influenza, and all other causes of death.

Despite many recent advances in the control and prevention of heart disease, it is still the number one killer in the developed world. Unlike most other diseases, heart attacks are sudden, often striking their victims so quickly that they do not have time to get medical help. The key to survival and recovery from a heart attack is learning to recognize early signs of heart disease. By seeking help early, victims can make their heart attacks much less threatening. People can also lessen heart attack risk by adopting a healthier life-style.

Sometimes the heart is thought of as a "motor" that runs the "machine" called the human body. In real machines, a mistake in the manufacturing process sometimes produces a faulty motor that does not run as well as it should. This is also true for the human heart, but these "manufacturing" mistakes are called congenital heart defects. With modern surgical techniques, many of these abnormalities can be repaired. Like a heavily used part of any machine, the heart can also "wear down" with age, although the harmful effects of many of these problems can be reduced by recognizing the problems early. Most machines whose motors break down can be fixed by replacing the old motor with a new one. In the past, it was not possible to replace a failing heart. However, one of the miracles of modern medicine is the ability of surgeons to replace a defective heart with a healthy one. Also in some cases a mechanical heart can be used as a temporary replacement for a diseased heart.

Heart disease is actually not a single ailment, but rather it is a group of diseases affecting various parts of the circulatory system, including the heart. The following chapters will explore how the human heart and circulatory system work and what happens when something goes wrong. They will also discuss related problems such as strokes and blood vessel disorders as well as the latest treatments for heart disease patients, factors that contribute to heart disease, and the ways that people can prevent and control this dreaded killer.

Heart disease is one of the most important health issues of our times. The more we learn about it, the better we will be able to cope with it and combat it.

CHAPTER

1

THE CIRCULATORY SYSTEM

If you run a race, become excited, or have a sudden fright, you can feel your heart thumping inside your chest. In times of stress, your heart works overtime to rush nutrients to where they are needed in your body. Most of the time, however, you don't notice your heart at all. Hour after hour, day after day, it contracts and relaxes about 70 times a minute as it pushes blood through your circulatory system. In an average lifetime, your heart will beat more than 2.5 billion times!

The Heart

The amazing organ called the heart is located between the lungs inside your chest. Shaped like a large, pointed egg, it is about the size of your fist. It is in the center of your torso, directly behind your breastbone, but because it is tipped slightly to the left, we sometimes think of it as being on the left side of the body.

From the time of the ancient Greeks, anatomists studied the heart and knew what it looked like, but it was not until the seventeenth century that they found out what purpose it served in the body. Then, in 1628, an English doctor, William Harvey, conducted a series of experiments that demonstrated for the first time that when the heart beats, it moves blood through our blood vessels.

The heart, illustrated in Figure 1, is a hollow, muscular chamber that functions like a pump, squeezing fluid through a series of pipes or tubes. The tubes to which it is connected are the veins and arteries, and the fluid that it pumps is blood. The inside of the heart is divided into two sides, each of which is divided into two smaller compartments. Each of the two upper compartments, which receive blood, is called an *atrium* or *auricle*. Blood moves from the atria (plural of "atrium") to the two lower compartments, which are called *ventricles*, and from there to the rest of the body. Between the upper and lower compartments and between the heart and the arteries are openings controlled by valves. The valves open to permit blood to flow through them, and close to cut off the blood flow.

The valves that control the openings between the atria and ventricles are called the *atrioventricular valves*. The one on the right side of the heart is formed by three flaps of tissue and is called the *tricuspid valve*. The one on the left has only two flaps and is called the *bicuspid*, or *mitral*, *valve*. It is smaller and stronger and able to resist the higher pressure on the left side

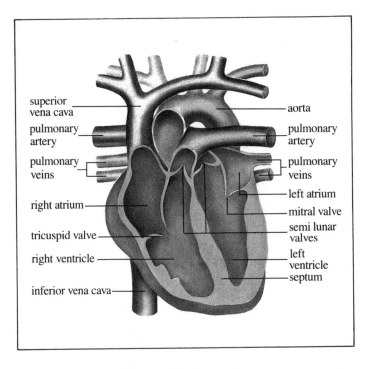

Figure 1. The human heart

of the heart. When the heart muscle relaxes, the flaps of the valves fall forward and allow the blood to pass through. When the heart contracts, blood rushes upward and pushes the flaps closed.

The valves at the openings to the aorta and pulmonary artery are called *semilunar valves* because they are shaped like small half-moons. When the heart contracts, these valves open as blood pushes against them, allowing blood to pass into the arteries. Blood flows forward through the circulatory system in one direction and is prevented by the valves from flowing backward.

Through the center of the heart is a vertical wall called the *septum* which divides the heart into two parts. The right side of the heart receives blood from the body and sends it to the lungs. The blood then returns from the lungs to the left side of the heart where it is pumped to the rest of the body. Blood is the body's transport system. It carries oxygen and nutrients to body cells and removes waste products that the cells do not need. The heart and the vessels by which the blood travels through the body form the circulatory system.

The Blood Vessels

As Figure 2 shows, the circulatory system is like a series of tiny, tubular rivers inside the body. If you could lay out all your blood vessels from end to end, they would be about 60,000 miles (96,560 km) long, or nearly two and a half times the distance around the equator!

Blood begins its journey from the heart through large vessels called *arteries*. The *pulmonary artery* leaves the right ventricle of the heart and divides into two branches. One of the branches goes to the left lung, and the other to the right lung. The blood returns from the lungs to the left side of the heart through the *pulmonary veins*. The blood is then pumped from the left ventricle to the rest of the body, leaving the heart through a large artery called the *aorta*. The aorta quickly branches into many smaller arteries leading to the head, trunk, arms, and legs.

Like every other part of the body, the heart itself

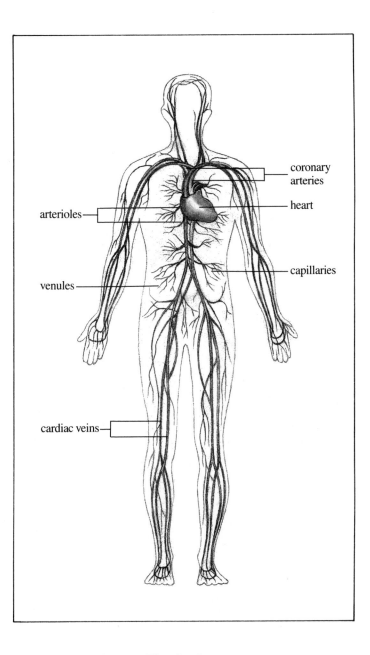

coronary
arteries

heart

arterioles

capillaries

venules

cardiac veins

Figure 2. The circulatory system

needs a steady blood supply and this comes from a dense network of arteries and veins on its surface. Ten percent of the blood pumped by the heart goes to these vessels. The first large arteries that branch off the aorta are called the *coronary arteries*. They supply the heart with the blood it needs. *Cardiac veins* bring blood back to the heart.

Throughout the body the arteries branch again and again until they become very small. At that point they are called *arterioles*. The arterioles branch into even smaller tubes called *capillaries*. Most of our blood vessels are capillaries. Capillaries are so small that they can be seen only under a microscope, and they are so narrow that only a single blood cell can squeeze through a capillary at a time. Nearly every body cell is in contact with at least one capillary. Capillary walls are thin and allow the blood to release oxygen and nutrients through them to the cells and to pick up waste products from the cells.

As blood flows back toward the heart, the capillaries join to form bigger and bigger tubes. The vessels that return blood to the heart are called *veins*. As blood flows toward the heart, the veins increase in size. The smallest veins are called *venules*. The largest veins are those that enter the heart. These are the *inferior vena cava*, which empties blood into the heart from the lower body, and the *superior vena cava*, which brings blood from the upper body.

Most of your large arteries are buried deep within the body. As for veins, however, if you look on the inside of your wrist or the back of your hand you can see some of them close to the surface of the skin.

Blood

As mentioned, blood is the body's transport system. It brings to the body cells everything they need for growth and repair and takes away waste products. Blood also contains cells that fight disease, and carries substances that repair injured parts of the body.

Blood is made up of both liquid and solid parts. The liquid part, called *plasma,* is colorless and surrounds the solid blood parts: *red corpuscles, white corpuscles,* and *platelets.* Red corpuscles, or red blood cells, form more than 90 percent of your blood cells and give the blood its red color. These cells look like tiny doughnuts without holes and are so small that each drop of blood contains 250 million of them.

Red blood cells contain *hemoglobin,* a compound made from iron. Hemoglobin combines readily with oxygen, which it picks up from the air (which has been breathed into the lungs) as the blood passes through the lungs. As the blood circulates through the body and comes into contact with cells that need oxygen, the hemoglobin releases the oxygen. Oxygen turns hemoglobin and the red corpuscles carrying the hemoglobin a bright red. Without oxygen, the red cells are darker. The reason the blood in your veins appears blue through your skin is that the veins carry blood that has given up its oxygen. If you cut yourself, and sever a vein, however, the blood that flows from your wound appears red again because the hemoglobin combines with oxygen in the air.

White corpuscles, or white blood cells, are large, shapeless cells whose primary purpose is to destroy

This illustration (based on a scanning electron micrograph) shows various blood cells escaping from a severed vein (top right).

harmful bacteria within the body. White blood cells can change their shape and when one comes in contact with a bacterium, it surrounds and digests it. Usually there is only about one white blood cell for every 800 red blood cells, but if you get sick or have an infection, your body increases the number of white blood cells to fight the germs causing the disease. White blood cells play a variety of roles in the body's immune system, including fighting viruses, poisons, and other foreign substances in the body.

Platelets are tiny particles that help the blood to clot. If you get a cut, blood flows out of the wound. When the blood is exposed to the air, the platelets form substances that combine with other elements in the plasma to form *fibrin,* a network of tiny, yellow threadlike structures that trap the blood and form a *clot,* or *thrombus.* Usually, blood clots form to prevent blood from leaking from a damaged vessel, but they may also form in a vessel damaged from within by disease or inflammation. If clots break free in the bloodstream, they may cause blockages in other parts of the circulatory system and prevent the flow of blood to that area. If, for instance, a clot blocked blood vessels going to the brain, the person would have a stroke. (The definition and causes of strokes are explained in Chapter 4.)

The Heartbeat

Each artery has a thick, muscular wall that expands as blood is driven into it by the heart and relaxes when the pressure is reduced between heartbeats. These expansions and contractions are what you feel when you take your pulse. They occur at the same time and at the same rate as your heartbeat.

Each heartbeat is a complex series of muscle contractions. Each contraction pushes about 70 milliliters (5 tablespoons) of blood into the circulatory system. The body has about 5 liters (5.5 quarts) of blood in it, and it takes about a minute for a blood cell to make one round trip through the circulatory system.

Although you can hear someone's heartbeat by pressing your ear against the person's chest, a doctor usually listens to the heart with a *stethoscope,* a device that magnifies the sound. You can magnify the sound somewhat without a stethoscope by listening through a cardboard tube. When you listen to a heartbeat, you hear two distinct parts—a longer, booming sound followed by a shorter, snapping sound—lub-dup, lub-dup, lub-dup. These are the sounds of the valves closing after blood has been pumped through them.

A heartbeat begins as the atria contract and push blood into the ventricles. The ventricles then contract and push blood into the arteries. The "lub" of each heartbeat is made when the ventricle contracts and the valve between the atrium and ventricle closes; the "dup" occurs when the valve between the ventricle and the artery closes. The part of the heartbeat cycle when the heart is contracting is called the *systole;* the part when it relaxes is called the *diastole.* The heart fills up with blood during the diastolic phase.

An average adult heart beats about 70 times a minute, although this can vary. Women often have

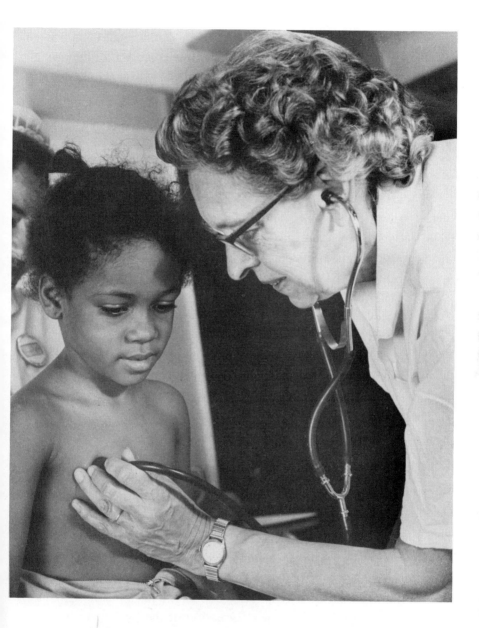

A doctor checks a young patient's heartbeat with a stethoscope.

faster heart rates than men, and children usually have faster rates than adults. In general, people with larger body sizes have lower heart rates. A baby, before it is born, has a heart rate of about 140 beats per minute, whereas a child's rate is about 90 beats per minute.

Many things can affect the heart rate. The heart slows down when we sleep or rest. During heavy exercise it is not unusual for the heart to beat up to 150 times per minute. (Well-trained athletes, on the other hand, can exercise without greatly raising their heart rate because their hearts pump more blood with each beat.) Activity or excitement also makes the heart beat faster. When you are excited or afraid, the body produces a chemical called *adrenaline*. Among other things, adrenaline stimulates the heart to beat faster, and this helps to bring nutrients to the body more quickly. This is sometimes called the "fight or flight" response because it helps the body to react quickly in times of stress.

Most of the muscles in the body are controlled by nerves connected to the brain. The muscles contract when the brain tells them to by sending a message along a nerve. The heart is unique in that it does not need directions from the brain in order to contract. It has its own control center, called the *pacemaker* or the *sinus node*. The pacemaker is formed by a special group of nerve cells located on the wall of the right atrium. When the cells of the pacemaker signal, they stimulate the contraction of the heart's atria. As the electric impulse of the nerve passes from the atria to the ventricles, it goes through another structure called the *atrioventricular node*. This acts something like a relay station. It slightly delays the impulse and then sends it on to the ventricles, signaling them to contract. The pacemaker acts like a sparkplug in a car engine, triggering a series of actions of the heart.

Although the heart does have its own control system, the rate set by the pacemaker can be changed somewhat by impulses from the nervous system and hormones from the endocrine system. Sensory receptors in various parts of the circulatory system detect blood pressure levels and send messages to the cardiac centers in the brain to speed the heart rate or to slow it down. Hormones produced in the adrenal and thyroid glands can also affect the heart rate as can temperature and emotions.

The heart rate is controlled in the brain by your *autonomic nervous system*. Unlike the nerves that you use when walking or talking, the *autonomic nerves* are not under voluntary control. You cannot will your heart to speed up or slow down in the same way that you can choose to bend or straighten your arm. However, when you are frightened or angry, the autonomic nerves stimulate the heart to speed up. When you are asleep, they signal the heart to slow down. The autonomic nerves control the body functions that keep you alive.

CHAPTER

2

DEFECTS OF THE HEART

Most of us are born with hearts that function normally. Sometimes, however, a baby's heart does not develop properly and the child is born with a congenital, or inborn, heart defect. Every year in the United States, about 25,000 babies are born with heart defects. Occasionally these defects disappear with age, and many of them can be repaired with surgery so that the patients can go on to lead normal lives. About 520,000 Americans have heart defects.

Doctors do not know why most heart defects occur. Sometimes the development of the baby is adversely affected if the mother has a viral disease such as German measles during her pregnancy. Drinking of excess alcohol by pregnant women is also linked to heart defects in their babies. People born with Down's syndrome, a condition which results from an abnormal number of chromosomes, sometimes have heart problems as well.

There are about thirty-five different kinds of recognized congenital heart defects. Heart defects range from barely noticeable malformations to life-threatening problems. In the U.S. alone, there are about 6,000 deaths each year caused by heart defects. Most defects are variations on, or combinations of, the following types.

Defects of the Aorta

When a baby is in the womb, its heart, like ours, is pumping blood throughout its body. However, before birth, the baby does not breathe air through its lungs as we do. Instead, it receives oxygen from its mother's blood through an organ called the *placenta*. Thus, until the baby is born, there is no need for the heart to pump blood to the lungs. Before birth, a baby has a small blood vessel called the *ductus arteriosus* which links the aorta with the pulmonary artery, thus allowing the blood to bypass the lungs. Normally, this passageway closes within a few weeks after the baby is born. If it does not close, some of the blood coming out of the heart in the aorta leaks into the ductus arteriosus and returns to the lungs instead of being circulated through the body. Then less oxygenated blood is available to the body. When the body tissues do not receive enough oxygen, the child tires easily. A surgeon can easily repair this defect, called patent ductus arteriosus, by cutting or tying the duct to close it. (See Figure 2-1.)

In a problem called coarctation of the aorta, the aorta has not formed properly and becomes very narrow at one point, which slows down the flow of blood.

(Blood, like any other liquid, flows more easily through a large tube than a small one.) Usually, this problem can be solved surgically. The surgeon removes the narrow section of the artery and either adds a new section or simply reconnects the remaining two parts of the artery by fastening their ends together.

Defects of the Heart Wall

Normally, there is no direct link between the right half and left half of the heart. Occasionally, however, the baby's heart develops with an opening between the two ventricles or the two atria, a condition sometimes called a "hole in the heart." Because the pressure is greater on the left side of the heart, some of its oxygen-rich blood leaks into the right side and is pumped to the lungs again. In order to pump enough blood through the body, the heart has to work harder. Like any muscle that is heavily stressed, a heart which has to work harder may become enlarged. Such a condition is not healthy because eventually the enlarged heart cannot work hard enough and fails to supply the body with enough blood.

Small openings in the heart wall often close themselves as the child develops. Large openings always require surgery. Sometimes the sides of the hole can be sewn together, or, if the hole is too large, a cloth patch can be used to close it.

Multiple Defects

Sometimes more than one malformation occurs at the same time. A defect called the tetralogy of Fallot, named after the doctor who first recognized it, is actually a combination of four abnormalities: (1) a large hole between the right and left ventricle, (2) a narrowing of the artery near the pulmonary valve, (3) an abnormally muscular right ventricle, and (4) the location of the aorta directly over the opening in the heart wall.

The blood of a baby with tetralogy of Fallot does not have enough oxygen. The blood therefore appears to be dark and makes the baby look blue around the lips and fingernails, a condition called *cyanosis*. The child may become tired and short of breath even during mild exercise. In most cases, surgery can repair the defects.

Defects in the Heart Valves

If any of the four valves in the heart develops improperly, the flow of blood will be obstructed. If the obstruction is severe, and the blood does not receive enough oxygen, the baby's skin may appear slightly blue. Whether surgery is needed depends on the location or degree of obstruction. A surgeon can enlarge a too-small valve opening to allow more blood to flow through. Sometimes it becomes necessary to insert an artificial heart valve.

Abnormalities in the Heart Rate

As mentioned, when you are excited or exercising, the number of times your heart beats per minute goes up; when you are sleeping, your heart rate goes down. These are normal fluctuations. Sometimes, however, the heart rate will speed up, slow down, or beat abnormally for no apparent reason. Any kind of abnormal rhythm is called an *arrhythmia*. An arrhythmia can occur at any age and does not necessarily indicate a problem.

The most common kind of arrhythmia occurs when the electrical stimulus for a heartbeat begins in an area other than the sinus node and causes the heart to beat early. This premature beat causes a slight delay before the next regular beat, which then becomes more forceful. Premature beats are common in normal children, who often outgrow them. Even when they continue, they usually pose no problem.

A heart rate that is too fast is called *tachycardia*. Whether a person's heart rate is too fast depends on age and physical activity. For instance, a teenager whose resting heartbeat is more than 100 beats a minute may have tachycardia. Yet, during exercise a teenager may normally have a heartbeat of more than 200 beats a minute.

The most common type of abnormally fast heart rate is called paroxysmal atrial tachycardia. The fast rate begins in the upper chambers of the heart and, in a baby, can produce a heart rate of more than 220 beats per minute. Tachycardia also can result when the electrical pathway between the atria and ventricles is abnormal and allows the signal to arrive at the ventricles too soon. Usually this condition can be controlled with drugs, although occasionally surgery is necessary. Sometimes a patient can learn special exercises to slow the heart.

Ventricular tachycardia, a serious condition in which the heartbeat begins in the ventricles rather than the atria, is caused by disease or injury to the heart. It usually needs to be treated promptly, either with drugs or by treating the underlying cause.

When the heart beats too slowly, the condition is called *bradycardia*. Again, the question of what is too slow depends on the individual. A normal resting heart rate for an athletically trained teenager may be 50 beats a minute, whereas a newborn usually has a resting heartbeat of 100 beats per minute. In a condition called sick sinus syndrome, the heartbeat is too slow because the pacemaker, or sinus node, fails or does not work fast enough. Then, not enough blood flows to the body organs and the person becomes excessively tired. Sick sinus syndrome sometimes occurs after open heart surgery.

A solution to the sick sinus syndrome is to implant an artificial pacemaker in the body. This device produces a small amount of electricity which stimulates the heart and keeps it from being too slow. An artificial pacemaker consists of a wire attached at one end to the heart wall, and at the other end to a control and battery unit. The control and battery unit are placed just under the skin of either the belly or the chest. Once in place, the pacemaker is unnoticeable, and the battery can be checked easily and painlessly from outside the body.

Occasionally, the heart's electric signal fails to flow along its normal pathway, a condition called heart block. This may occur as the result of disease or after heart surgery. When the electric pathway is blocked,

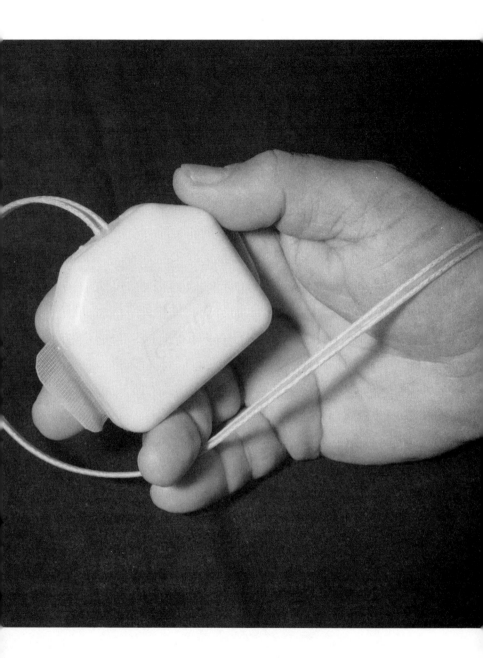

An artificial pacemaker

the atria and ventricles beat independently. Sometimes children are born with heart block and have no problem. However, when heart block develops later in life, the patient often needs an artificial pacemaker to regulate the heartbeat's rate and keep it from becoming too slow.

CHAPTER

3

INFECTIONS THAT AFFECT
THE HEART

The common cold is a typical infectious disease—tiny
cold germs enter your body and cause a variety of
symptoms that may include a runny nose, cough, and
sometimes a fever. Most people feel terrible during
the time they are sick, but, as in most infectious diseases, once they have recovered, there are no aftereffects.

Some infectious diseases, however, are more
dangerous and can have lasting effects which may in-
volve permanent damage to the heart. These diseases
include *rheumatic fever, bacterial endocarditis, Kawasaki disease,* and *pericarditis.*

Rheumatic Fever

If you have ever had a bad sore throat, you probably
went to the doctor and had a throat culture taken in
which the doctor or nurse briefly rubbed a cotton swab

on the back of your throat. A few of the germs causing the sore throat were picked up by the swab and then placed on a specially prepared laboratory dish to grow. If the germs were identified as being those of a bacterium called *Streptococcus,* then you had what is commonly called a strep throat. Symptoms of strep throat include a sudden sore throat (especially one in which it is painful to swallow), fever, swollen glands under the jaw, headache, and sometimes nausea and vomiting.

Luckily, a strep throat can be treated easily with antibiotics. This is important because if not treated it can develop into a more dangerous disease called rheumatic fever. Rheumatic fever can affect many parts of the body including the heart, joints, brain, and skin. In 1985, 6,200 Americans died of rheumatic fever and rheumatic heart disease. Of the more than 2 million people now living who have had rheumatic fever, many suffer from permanent heart damage. Rheumatic fever typically occurs in children five to fifteen years old, but its effects can last for the rest of the person's life.

Rheumatic fever usually begins with a high fever lasting from ten days to two weeks. If the joints are infected they may be very painful, and if the heart is infected the patient may experience shortness of breath or chest pains. There may also be a loss of appetite and unusual fatigue. A doctor can determine whether or not a patient's heart has been injured by rheumatic fever by looking at an *electrocardiogram* (see chapter 8). Some children who have suffered heart damage from rheumatic fever have to limit their participation in certain kinds of sports or other strenuous activities.

The main problem with rheumatic fever is that it can cause permanent damage to the heart valves by creating a situation in which a valve either only partially closes or partially opens. When a valve does not close properly (a condition called insufficiency), some of the blood leaks back into the heart chamber from which it was pumped and mixes with the blood that was just emptied into the chamber. This larger amount of blood puts an extra strain on the heart muscle the next time it contracts. If a valve does not open widely enough (a condition called stenosis), the heart must work harder than usual to push blood through the narrow opening. In this case, too, the heart is put under a strain.

Many people with damaged heart valves have no noticeable symptoms for many years. Eventually, though, the extra strain on the heart can cause a variety of problems.

A heart in which the valves on the left side leak, gradually enlarges to help pump the increased amount of blood. When the heart becomes enlarged as a result of rheumatic heart disease, it needs an increased blood supply. If the coronary arteries do not supply enough blood, the person may experience chest pains, dizziness or fainting during exercise, shortness of breath, and tiredness or palpitations.

Heart valves that have been badly damaged by rheumatic fever can be replaced through surgery with either artificial valves or valves from an animal such as a pig. Most people with substitute valves improve significantly.

The streptococcus bacterium also causes other

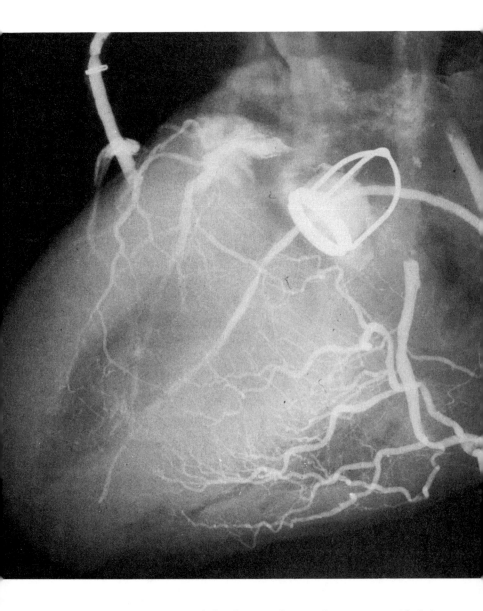

This X-ray image of the human heart shows an artificial aortic heart valve. A normal aortic valve controls the flow of blood pumped from the heart's left ventricle.

kinds of illness, including scarlet fever. The best prevention for rheumatic heart disease is to get prompt treatment for any kind of streptococcus infection so that it does not spread to the heart.

Bacterial Endocarditis

Bacterial endocarditis is a serious infection of the heart valves or tissues lining the heart. It does not occur often, but it is a particular danger to people who already have abnormalities in the structure of their hearts, who have artificial heart valves, or who have undergone certain kinds of heart surgery. In 1985, 20,000 Americans were hospitalized with bacterial endocarditis.

Bacteria is present in the bloodstream all the time. Normally, they are destroyed by the body's defense system. Sometimes, however, they lodge on an abnormal or artificial heart valve, where they grow and multiply and cause damage to the surrounding tissue. For people who have abnormal or artificial heart valves, antibiotics can be used to fight the bacteria and extra care can be taken to prevent bacteria from entering the bloodstream, especially during any kind of dental work or surgery.

Kawasaki Disease

Kawasaki disease, sometimes called mucocutaneous lymph node syndrome, is a relatively rare illness, usually affecting children under the age of five. Typical symptoms are fever, a rash, swelling of the hands and feet, irritated eyes, swollen glands, and irritation and inflammation of the mouth, lips, and throat. The symptoms normally last ten days to two weeks and usually the child fully recovers. In about one-fifth of all cases, however, there is damage to the coronary arteries or heart muscle, although usually the damaged areas heal within five to six weeks.

Kawasaki disease has probably been around for a long time, although it was recognized as a separate disease only in 1967 by a Japanese pediatrician, Dr. Tomisaku Kawasaki, after whom it is named. The disease occurs more often in Japan than in any other country and nearly twice as often in boys as in girls. In the United States, Kawasaki disease usually occurs in children of Asian ancestry. No one knows the cause of the disease, but a virus is strongly suspected.

Pericarditis

The heart is held in place inside the chest by a tough two-layer coat called the *pericardium*. An infection of this tissue is called *pericarditis*. It causes a pain in the chest and a change in the heart's electrocardiogram pattern. And a doctor listening to the heartbeat through a stethoscope hears a slight rubbing sound caused by the two layers of the pericardium scraping against each other.

As the heart expands and contracts during each heartbeat, it normally slides over the smooth inner layer of the pericardium. However, in some cases of pericarditis, the inflammation damages the pericardium, which is then replaced with a tough scar tissue around the heart. This condition, which is called constrictive pericarditis, prevents the heart from expanding fully during its relaxation phase. Usually, the scar tissue can be removed surgically and the heart can function without that part of the pericardium.

Pericarditis can also produce a condition called pericardial effusion in which too much fluid accumulates between the two pericardial layers. This puts pressure on the heart and prevents it from filling up completely with blood. In such cases, a doctor must immediately drain some of the fluid so that the heart can beat freely again.

Pericarditis may be caused by infection, physical injury, harmful substances in the blood, radiation, or tumors. It also sometimes occurs with rheumatic fever and some forms of arthritis.

CHAPTER

4

BLOOD PRESSURE

The American Heart Association estimates that 58 million American adults and children have high blood pressure or are being treated for it. Although most cases are mild, about 30,000 people die from it each year, and many more die of heart attacks or strokes in which high blood pressure is the major contributing factor. What is high blood pressure, and why is it so dangerous?

Measuring Blood Pressure

As the heart contracts, the blood inside is squeezed and put under pressure. The force necessary to push the blood out of a heart and through the arteries is known as *blood pressure*. Blood pressure is the measure of how much pressure is being exerted by blood on artery walls. The harder and faster the heart beats, the higher the blood pressure.

(43)

To measure your blood pressure, the doctor or nurse wraps a wide band called a *sphygmomanometer* around your upper arm. As air is pumped into the band, it applies pressure and prevents the flow of blood through the arteries of the arm. The pressure is slowly released, and by listening through a stethoscope, the doctor or nurse can hear when blood begins to flow again.

We measure two kinds of blood pressure; one is measured when the heart is contracting, and the other when it is relaxing. The contracting, or systolic, pressure is higher than the relaxing, or diastolic, pressure. Usually, blood pressure is given as a fraction. A typical blood pressure, for instance, is 120/80. This means that the systolic pressure was strong enough to raise a column of mercury 120 millimeters high and it fell to 80 millimeters during diastole. Blood pressure can go up when you exercise, when you become excited, or when you get chilled. In general, blood pressure goes up with age, the systolic pressure ranging from about 40 in a newborn baby to 140 in a sixty-year-old. Although normal pressure varies with each individual, a general measure of high blood pressure is anything above 140 over 90 in a healthy adult.

Regulating Blood Pressure

The body regulates blood pressure in a variety of ways. With each heartbeat, the arteries expand as they receive blood from the heart and then contract as the blood moves into the capillaries and veins. As in any

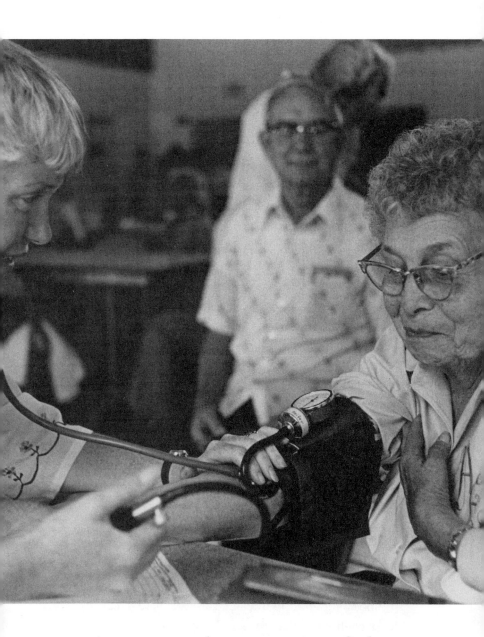

*A nurse uses a sphygmomanometer to check
a patient's blood pressure.*

system of pipes or tubes, the larger the outlet, the easier it is for the liquid to flow out. The changes in the size of the small arteries to control the speed of the blood running into capillaries and veins in turn change the amount of pressure being exerted by the blood in the big arteries. (Blood pressure is normally measured in the big arteries.)

Blood pressure is also regulated by the kidneys. The kidneys have special structures that can detect changes in blood pressure. When the pressure falls too low, the kidneys release a substance called *renin* into the blood. Through a series of chemical changes, the renin causes the small arteries to close, thus increasing the blood pressure. In another series of reactions, the renin acts on the adrenal glands, a pair of glands that lie just above the kidneys, and causes them to release a substance called *aldosterone*. Aldosterone causes the kidneys to retain sodium, and this retention of sodium signals the body to retain more water. When there is more water in the body, there is more fluid in the blood vessels and the blood pressure rises. Blood pressure is also regulated by substances produced in the brain and within the heart itself.

The Silent Killer

Although high blood pressure is sometimes linked to problems such as kidney abnormalities or tumors on an adrenal gland, in most cases the actual cause of the high blood pressure is unknown. In general, high blood pressure is associated with age. As a person gets older, the likelihood of high blood pressure increases. The tendency to have high blood pressure is inherited, so that if your parents have it, you are more likely to develop it as well. You are also more likely to have high blood pressure if you are overweight or eat too much salt. Race is another factor associated with blood pressure. Black Americans are two to three times more likely to have high blood pressure than white Americans.

The medical term for high blood pressure is *hypertension.* Although the term does not mean that the person is tense, there is an association between stress and high blood pressure. Under stress, the adrenal glands tend to produce substances that contribute to high blood pressure.

High blood pressure is sometimes called the silent killer because a person can have it for a long time without any apparent ill effects. The danger of high blood pressure is that by forcing the heart to pump with greater force, it puts it under a strain that eventually becomes too great for the heart to bear. When the heart is forced to work harder than usual over a long period of time, it tends to enlarge. Eventually, however, it can no longer enlarge so it fails to be able to supply enough blood to the body. As a result, the blood backs up in the system so it cannot get rid of waste or pick up oxygen quickly enough.

High blood pressure also damages the blood vessels and causes them to become scarred, hardened, and less elastic. When the heart cannot pump hard enough and the arteries become inflexible or too narrowed, then the body is not supplied with an adequate amount of blood and the nutrients the blood carries. Without sufficient nutrients, the body parts cannot function properly. All these conditions lead to the possibility of heart failure.

High blood pressure is the most important factor in causing strokes. The higher the blood pressure, the more likely a person is to have a stroke. When the arteries become hardened or narrowed it becomes easier for a blood clot to become lodged in an artery and block the blood flow. In the last decade, the number of deaths from stroke has significantly decreased, chiefly because a greater awareness of the role of high blood pressure has influenced people to seek treatment or to change their life-styles.

High blood pressure can be combatted in a variety of ways, which include using medically prescribed drugs, controlling diet and weight, and exercising. Many kinds of drugs are used to lower blood pressure. Some work by ridding the body of extra salts and fluids. Others reduce the heart rate and the flow of blood from the heart. Some drugs prevent the arteries from constricting too much.

In some cases of mild hypertension, drugs are not necessary. Simply changing to a low-salt diet is enough to reduce blood pressure. Overweight people can often lower their blood pressure by losing weight. In a recent study done in Australia, it was found that periodic exercise alone can reduce high blood pressure in some people. Every case is different, and it is important for the individual to consult a doctor for proper treatment.

Low Blood Pressure

Sometimes people wonder if there can be a problem with a blood pressure that is too low. Such a condition does not exist. As long as the heart is beating and providing the body with an adequate amount of blood, the blood pressure is sufficient even if it is low.

A low blood pressure may be quite normal, and normality depends on the age, race, sex, and environment of the individual. For instance, low blood pressure is more common in young people than in the elderly, and in oriental than occidental persons. In a recent insurance company survey, it was found that the people with the lowest blood pressures tended to live the longest.

Strokes

Every year, about half a million Americans suffer from strokes, and of these, nearly one-third die. After heart attacks and cancer, strokes are the third leading cause of death in the United States as well as a major cause of disability.

Strokes are a result of a cardiovascular disease that affects the arteries in and leading to the brain. A stroke occurs when one of these arteries either breaks or becomes blocked so that the brain's supply of oxygen and nutrients is cut off. Without oxygen, brain cells die almost immediately; when those cells stop functioning, the body parts controlled by that part of the brain no longer work either. Because the brain

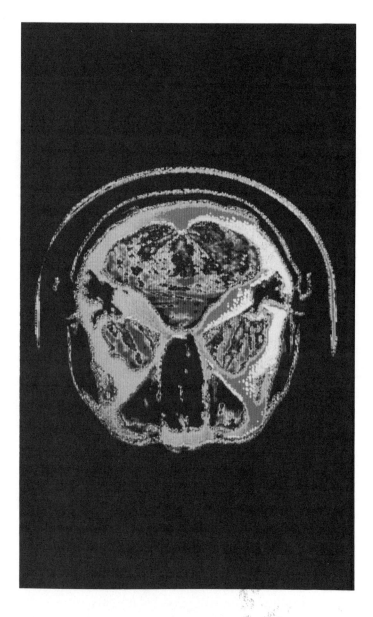

A continuous X ray, or CAT scan, of the human brain following a stroke

cannot replace dead brain cells, there is often permanent loss of some body functions in those people who survive a stroke.

Each part of the brain controls a different part of the body, so, depending on which part of the brain is affected, the aftereffects of a stroke will differ. The right half of the brain affects the left side of the body as well as language and some memory skills. The left half of the brain controls the right half of the body as well as spatial and perceptual skills. If a stroke on one side of the brain has paralyzed half of the body, the condition is called *hemiplegia.*

The most common type of stroke is called a *cerebral thrombosis,* and it occurs when a clot forms inside an artery that brings blood to the brain. Usually these are arteries that have been damaged by *atherosclerosis,* or hardening of the arteries. This type of stroke usually occurs at night or early in the morning, when blood pressure in the body is low, thus allowing blood clots to thicken without much resistance.

Some people who have this type of stroke have previously had ''ministrokes,'' smaller strokes called *transient ischemic attacks,* or *TIAs.* A TIA occurs when a blood clot temporarily blocks an artery and then breaks loose again. Most TIAs last less than five minutes and usually do not have permanent aftereffects. Indications of a TIA include temporary weakness; clumsiness or loss of feeling in an arm, leg, or the side of the face; temporary loss of vision in one eye; or temporary loss of speech or difficulty in speaking or understanding speech. Sometimes there is also dizziness, double vision, or staggering. A TIA is a warning signal that a full-fledged stroke could occur sometime in the future and requires prompt medical attention.

A stroke can also take place when a blood clot that forms away from the brain is carried there through an artery. This kind of stroke is called a *cerebral embolism*. The usual source of these wandering blood clots is the heart. When a condition called atrial *fibrillation* occurs in the heart, the heart quivers all over instead of producing a steady beat and it fails to pump all of the blood out of the chambers with each heartbeat. The pooled blood that remains in the heart tends to clot, and, if the clots circulate in the body, they can get lodged in an artery that supplies the brain with blood.

Strokes can also occur when a blood vessel breaks, either on the surface of the brain or within the brain itself. Again, the inadequate supply of blood to brain cells means that that part of the brain cannot function.

The likelihood of having a stroke increases with age, especially after the age of fifty-five. Nearly three-quarters of all people who have strokes are over sixty-five. Men as a group have more strokes than women, and black Americans have more than white Americans. People who are most likely to have strokes are those that have high blood pressure, heart disease, and diabetes mellitus, as well as those who have a personal or family history of strokes.

Strokes can also occur when a blood vessel in or on the surface of the brain bursts. This form of stroke, called a cerebral hemorrhage, causes brain cells normally nourished by the broken artery to be deprived of their blood supply. Accumulated blood can also put pressure on surrounding brain tissue and cause problems. The bursting of an aneurysm, a blood-filled balloon on the wall of an artery, can also cause a stroke and impaired brain function.

CHAPTER

5

DISEASES OF THE HEART AND BLOOD VESSELS

As a woman climbed up a steep hill, her heart began to pound and her breath came in increasingly quicker gasps. In a neighboring park, a middle-aged man playing tennis suddenly clutched his chest and collapsed in a heap. Elsewhere, an elderly man died quietly in his sleep. All of these people suffered from some form of heart or circulatory system disease.

Atherosclerosis

As we get older, our bodies become less flexible, and some thickening and hardening of the arteries is normal. The general term for this process is *arteriosclerosis.* The type of arteriosclerosis that often leads to heart attacks is called *atherosclerosis* from the Greek words *athero,* which means gruel or paste, and *sclerosis,* which means hardness. In atherosclerosis, pasty deposits of fats, *cholesterol,* cellular waste products, calcium, and fibrin become attached to the inner walls of the arteries. These accumulated substances are called *plaque*. Like the mineral deposits that clog up old water pipes, plaque obstructs the flow of blood through the arteries by making them narrower and less elastic. When there is a plaque buildup, there are two potential problems: (1) the blood vessel may bleed at the site of the plaque, or (2) a blood clot may form on the plaque's surface. Either of these can lead to a heart attack or stroke.

Atherosclerosis usually affects the large and medium-size arteries. It develops slowly and may begin early in life. Often a person is not aware that it has occurred until there is considerable plaque buildup. Scientists do not know exactly what causes cells to begin to build up on the artery wall although many believe it starts when the artery wall becomes damaged. In places where the artery wall is damaged, blood platelets accumulate. Blood platelets can form blood clots, and if this happens, the artery may be blocked, stopping the normal blood flow.

Artery walls can become damaged when there are high levels of cholesterol and *triglycerides* in the blood, or when blood pressure is high, or as a result of cigarette smoking. Recently scientists have begun to better understand what roles these factors play in the body and how they can lead to heart attacks. Figure 3 shows how atherosclerosis and clotting can gradually damage the arteries.

Angina

When coronary arteries are filled with plaque, the amount of blood going to the heart is reduced and the

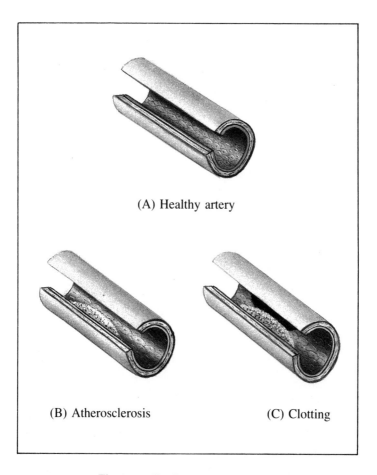

(A) Healthy artery

(B) Atherosclerosis   (C) Clotting

Figure 3. Cardiovascular disease:
the silent killer

High blood pressure, high cholesterol levels and other
factors may gradually lead to damaged arteries. Once
vital coronary vessels are clogged, a person can
suffer a heart attack. (A) The risk of heart failure is
usually low among young children, whose artery walls are
typically damage-free. (B) In a condition called
atherosclerosis, which can be caused by smoking and
high cholesterol, the arteries become lined with plaque.
(C) A clot forms on a tissue in the plaque. This shuts off
blood circulation in a coronary artery, causing a heart attack.

heart tissues do not receive as much oxygen as they need. This condition is called *myocardial ischemia.* *Ischemia* means the suppression of the flow of blood, which, in this case, is to the heart muscle. Under normal circumstances, the heart may be able to function adequately even with a reduced blood supply, but if put under stress, such as during physical exercise, it does not have enough oxygen to increase its output. The result is an attack of severe pains in the chest called *angina pectoris.* These may spread to the shoulder, arm and sometimes the jaw. Attacks of angina can be warnings of a possible future heart attack.

Many people suffer from ischemia without knowing it, a condition called *silent ischemia.* Even though their hearts may be deprived of blood for periods of time, they feel no pain. The American Heart Association estimates that there may be 3 to 4 million Americans with silent ischemia. Like people with angina, they may be subject to sudden heart attacks, but theirs come with no previous warning.

For some people who develop blocked coronary arteries, a back-up system takes over to continue supplying the heart with blood. Numerous small arteries connect the larger coronary arteries. Normally these remain closed, but if the coronary arteries become clogged, these vessels can open and provide a detour around the blockage and maintain the heart's blood supply.

People who suffer from angina can be treated with drugs that either help increase the supply of oxygen to the heart or reduce the heart's demand for oxygen. Sometimes clogged arteries can be opened up to improve the blood supply to the heart, but if the coronary arteries are severely blocked, surgery may be necessary to bypass the blockage.

Heart Attack

Every year one and a half million people in the United States suffer from heart attacks, and of these, half a million die. Nearly half of all heart attack victims are under the age of sixty-five and 5 percent are under the age of forty. Heart attack is the leading cause of death in America.

A heart attack occurs when the blood supply to the heart is reduced or stopped. Without nutrients, the heart muscle cannot work, and if the supply is cut off severely or for a long period of time, the heart muscle tissue becomes permanently damaged or dies. The medical term for a heart attack is *myocardial infarction,* which means death of the *myocardium,* or heart tissue. The severity of the heart attack depends on how much of the heart's blood supply has been cut off and for how long.

Atherosclerosis often leads to a heart attack when a clot forms in one of the arteries that supply the heart muscle with blood. Because a clot is also called a thrombus, this kind of heart attack is sometimes called a *coronary thrombosis* or a *coronary occlusion.* A heart attack can also occur if the blood supply to the heart is decreased because of a contraction or spasm in a coronary artery. The cause of such spasms is unknown, but they can occur in normal arteries or in those that are partially blocked.

A person having a heart attack can have a variety of symptoms. Usually there is a feeling of uncomfortable pressure, fullness, squeezing, or pain in the center of the chest that lasts two minutes or longer. Often the pain spreads to the shoulders, neck or arms and the person may feel dizzy, faint, sweaty, or experience nausea or shortness of breath. Immediate treatment is essential to prevent permanent heart damage or death.

Most people who die from heart attacks do so within two hours of the beginning of the attack, often because they do not seek help. Yet, if the victim gets help immediately, much of the damage can be dramatically avoided. Of those people who receive emergency care and survive, 80 percent are able to return to work within three months.

When a coronary artery becomes blocked, the heart tissue that is not receiving enough oxygen begins to die. Once it is gone it cannot regrow. However, if the blood flow to that area of the heart can be restored soon enough, the tissue can be saved. Several kinds of drugs are now used to dissolve blood clots, and if they are given soon after the onset of a heart attack, they can help prevent damage to the heart.

Some kinds of heart attacks result in sudden death. Such deaths are most shocking when they occur in young people, especially when they are star athletes who appear to be in top physical condition. In March 1990, Loyola Marymount star basketball player Hank Gathers was leading his team toward a championship. In a spectacular play, he scored a goal with a slam dunk; then, a minute later, while running back to the other end of the court, he collapsed and died. Like athlete Flo Hyman, who died in 1986 after collapsing in a volleyball match in Japan, and Larry Gordan, a Miami Dolphin football player, who died in 1983 while jogging, his heart suddenly failed. Doctors cite a variety of reasons ranging from genetic disorders to undetected blockage to explain sudden in young athletes. Even in people whose health are closely monitored, potential problems cannot always be predicted.

When the heart muscle is damaged, the normal rhythm of the heartbeat is sometimes disrupted. This can lead either to ventricular tachycardia, in which the heart develops a very fast, abnormal heartbeat and reduces the amount of blood pumped to the body, or to ventricular fibrillation, in which the beating becomes totally disorganized and irregular and no blood is pumped at all. In either case, if the regular rhythm is not restored immediately, death comes quickly. In such an emergency, the only way to restore normal blood flow is by using a device called a *defibrillator,* which gives an electric shock to the heart and stimulates the resumption of a normal beat, or by using CPR techniques.

Over half of the estimated 650,000 people who suffer fatal heart attacks each year die before they reach a hospital. Many of them might have survived if they had been given *cardiopulmonary resuscitation (CPR).* "Cardio" refers to the heart, "pulmonary" to the lungs, and "resuscitation" means to bring back to life.

A person is considered to be clinically dead the moment the heart stops beating and breathing stops.

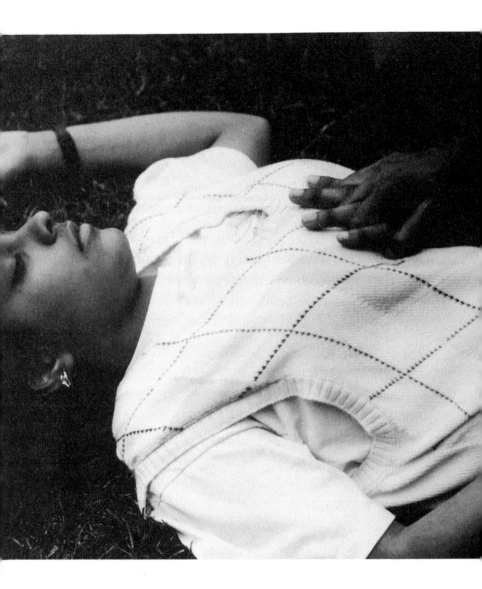

*Cardiopulmonary resuscitation, popularly
known as CPR, entails the application
of pressure on the patient's chest
to revive both the heart and lungs.*

When the heart no longer circulates blood through the body, life-giving oxygen is no longer carried to the body cells, including those in the brain. Brain cells die within four to six minutes after their oxygen supply has failed, and when that happens the person is considered to be biologically dead. CPR is a technique that can help a victim to breathe and circulate blood until the heart and lungs can resume those functions on their own.

CPR must be given immediately, and this is usually before paramedics or other emergency care people are able to arrive on the scene. Most communities offer classes that train people in CPR techniques, and as more people learn those techniques, more lives are saved. You can consult the Red Cross, the American Heart Association, your fire department, local hospital, or schools to find out when and where instruction is available in your community.

Congestive Heart Failure

Congestive heart failure occurs when the heart has been damaged and cannot pump enough blood to the body. High blood pressure, a heart attack, atherosclerosis, congenital heart defects, rheumatic fever, and high pressure in the lungs as a result of lung disease are all possible causes of damage to the heart. When the heart is damaged, it does not work as efficiently as it should and the system for transporting nutrients and removing body wastes is slowed down. As the blood flow slackens, the blood tends to back up in the veins.

Then fluids accumulate in the body tissues and swelling results. The most common indications of congestive heart failure are swelling in the legs or ankles and difficulty with breathing caused by fluid in the lungs.

People who suffer from congestive heart failure can be helped by rest, a proper diet, and modified daily activities. A number of drugs can also relieve many of the problems caused by the weakened heart. Digitalis, a drug derived from a plant called foxglove, works as a tonic and stimulates the pumping action of the heart. Other drugs, called *diuretics,* help the body rid itself of excess salts and fluids. Drugs called *vasodilators* are sometimes used to expand the blood vessels and make it easier for blood to flow through them. *Antihypertensives*, drugs that lower blood pressure, can also help people with congestive heart failure. With a combination of drugs and a controlled life-style, most people with congestive heart problems can continue to function relatively normally.

CHAPTER

6

CHOLESTEROL

One of the most heavily advertised features on many of today's foods is that they are low in *cholesterol* or have none at all. And some foods, such as oat bran, have recently been promoted as helping the body reduce its levels of this substance.

Cholesterol is one of the chief villains in the heart disease story. The more we know about it and how the body uses it, the better we will be able to understand how it has achieved this terrible reputation.

Cholesterol in the Body

Cholesterol is a yellow, fatty, waxlike substance that is found in eggs and animal fats, and is produced in the body from the foods we eat. During digestion, fats are broken down into tiny fat molecules called lipids. Lipids can also be formed from other nutrients, such as carbohydrates and protein. Lipids, which are also sometimes called "simple" fats, can be used by body cells to produce heat and energy. They are also used to construct more-complex fats such as cholesterol and lecithin, a process which takes place in the liver.

Cholesterol and lecithin are important in the functioning of the brain and nervous system. Cholesterol is also used to manufacture some hormones and vitamin D. It is also a source of bile acids and salts which are needed for digestion. Our bodies need cholesterol, but if we have too much and the body cannot get rid of it, it endangers our hearts.

In the body, cholesterol and other lipids combine with proteins to form substances called *lipoproteins* which travel through the bloodstream. Lipoproteins vary in the amount of cholesterol they carry and in size and weight. Low-density lipoproteins (LDLs) bring cholesterol from the liver to the body cells. If there is any extra cholesterol, it is deposited on the artery walls, where it forms *plaque*. Because plaque narrows the width of an artery and by so doing contributes to high blood pressure, LDLs are often refered to as the "bad cholesterol." High-density lipoproteins (HDLs) remove cholesterol from artery walls and also help to prevent it from being deposited in the first place. They are sometimes thought of as the "good cholesterol." Cholesterol is eliminated from the body in the form of bile acids and salts.

Cholesterol in the body is controlled by an enzyme called HMG reductase. The amount of this enzyme varies from one person to another and is one reason why people have different cholesterol levels.

A relatively high level of cholesterol in the body is not necessarily dangerous if the ratio of LDLs to HDLs shows a higher proportion of HDLs than normal. The average adult male has about five LDLs for each HDL.

Like other physical characteristics, your cholesterol levels are controlled in part by your genes. A high level of cholesterol in the blood is called *hypercholesterolemia*. Recently, a new group of drugs has been developed that can be used to lower cholesterol levels, but the best way to reduce body cholesterol is by altering your diet to one which is low in cholesterol and saturated fats.

A doctor can test your blood to measure your level of cholesterol. In general, a measurement of 200 milligrams per deciliter (mg/dl) is considered acceptable for a middle-aged person and suggests a low risk for heart disease. However, if the level rises to more than 240 mg/dl, then the likelihood of heart disease doubles. Nearly one-quarter of the people in the United States fall into this category.

The American Heart Association recommends that adults should be tested once every five years for both cholesterol and *triglycerides,* another group of fatty substances that contribute to heart disease and atherosclerosis. Triglycerides are used by the liver to produce LDLs.

Diet and Cholesterol

The average American diet is made up of at least 37 percent fat with a usual daily intake of 450 to 500 milligrams of cholesterol. A diet that is high in fat can lead to elevated cholesterol and triglyceride levels, particularly if it includes a high percentage of saturated fats. Animal fats such as butter, bacon grease, or those found in some red meats, are higher in saturated fats than are vegetable oils. Fat molecules, like other organic molecules, are made of long chains of atoms—primarily carbon, oxygen, and hydrogen. When some of the links in the chain have multiple bonds, the fat is said to be unsaturated. But if the links are partially broken and hydrogen atoms are added, the molecule becomes saturated with hydrogen, or hydrogenated.

Saturated, or hydrogenated, fats are more easily and completely digested by the body but they also contribute to higher cholesterol levels. Saturated fats are usually solid at room temperature and include butter, lard, and other animal fats. Good sources of unsaturated fats are corn, cottonseed, soya, and safflower oils. Sometimes food manufacturers add hydrogen atoms to unsaturated fats to keep them from spoiling. These fats are then partially hydrogenated. Monounsaturated fats such as olive and peanut oil have all their chemical bonds filled except for one. Polyunsaturated fats have many bonds available for the addition of hydrogen atoms.

Eggs, cheese, and liver are foods that contain the largest amounts of cholesterol, whereas skim milk and certain fishes contain little. Plant foods contain no cholesterol at all. The American Heart Association recommends that each person's daily intake of fat should be reduced to 30 percent of the total number of ingested calories and that cholesterol should be kept at about 300 milligrams per day. It also suggests that you choose lean cuts of meat, limit yourself to 5 to 7 ounces (142 to 198 g) of meat, poultry, or seafood each day, and use only low-fat dairy products. Some foods have actually been shown to help lower body cholesterol at least in some people. They include foods, such as oat bran, which tend to combine with bile salts produced by the liver and carry them out of the body. Foods containing vitamin C have also been shown to lower the levels of cholesterol and triglycerides in the blood. Vitamin C helps to remove cholesterol from the arteries and sends it to the liver, where it is changed into bile acids. Although eating such foods as oatmeal and orange juice may slightly lower your cholesterol count, the best way to keep your cholesterol level low is to eat a low-fat diet.

A recent study by a group of Canadian researchers showed that another way to reduce your body's cholesterol is to alter your eating patterns. They found that people who nibbled all day had a cholesterol level 13.5 percent lower than they did on a diet of the same foods eaten in three large meals. Normally, after eating a large meal, the body produces a large amount of insulin, a hormone that is essential for the body's processing of sugar. Insulin also stimulates the liver to produce cholesterol and causes changes in the artery walls that promote plaque formation. Nibblers, however, maintain a steady, but low, output of insulin. A diet of many small meals is one way to control cholesterol, but it can be impractical and is often a problem for people who have a tendency to overeat.

CHAPTER

7

RISK FACTORS FOR
HEART DISEASE

Every thirty-two seconds, or about the time it will take you to read this page, one more person will die from cardiovascular disease. Fortunately, many of these deaths can be prevented. Changes in life-style and eating and exercise patterns *can* significantly reduce the likelihood of a heart attack. In the United States, as people have become more aware of these factors, the number of people dying from heart disease has actually declined. Yet, we can do more. The best way to prevent heart disease is to be aware of the factors that contribute to it.

The three leading risk factors for developing heart disease are high blood pressure, elevated blood cholesterol levels, and cigarette smoking. If you fall into one or more of these categories, then your chances of becoming a heart disease victim go up sharply. The effects of obesity, diabetes, physical inactivity, and stress are less dramatic, but they too contribute to the possibility of heart disease. All of these factors are things that can be changed or treated to make your life healthier and reduce the danger of heart disease.

Age and Heredity

Some factors that contribute to the probability of heart disease, such as age, sex, and heredity, cannot be altered. Over half the people who have heart attacks and nearly 80 percent of those who die from them are over sixty-five. Thus, it is clear that the older you become, the more likely it is that you will suffer from heart disease. Although statistics also show that you are more likely to have a heart attack if you are male, the number of females having and dying from heart attacks is growing. Men are more prone to heart attacks in middle age, whereas women tend to have them after the age of sixty-five.

You may also be born with a tendency to have heart disease. Some families have an increased risk of heart disease, as do certain segments of the population. One of the routine questions asked by doctors at a physical checkup is whether the patient has a family history of heart disease. If your parents, grandparents, or other close relatives have suffered from heart attacks, atherosclerosis, or any other kind of cardiovascular disease, then you are more likely to develop heart disease than a person whose family has not experienced it.

We inherit our physical traits from our parents through tiny structures in the body cells called genes. Half of your genes are contributed by your mother, and half by your father. There are millions of genes in the body, each one affecting some part of a body process, and in some cases defective genes are responsible for diseases. It is believed that the tendency to develop heart disease is among the most common genetic defects.

One of these genetic diseases, called familial hypercholesterolemia (FH), affects about one in every 500 people in the United States. It is a hereditary ailment in which the victim has an elevated level of blood cholesterol. A child born with FH may have a cholesterol count as high as 1,000, nearly five times the normal cholesterol level. Although the heart is normal at birth, the enormous overload of cholesterol in the bloodstream causes atherosclerosis, which strains the heart and eventually triggers a heart attack.

If both parents have contributed an FH gene, the danger of heart attack is severe and may occur as early as the age of five. Such individuals usually do not live beyond the age of twenty. Luckily, only one person in a million is born with two FH genes. People with only one FH gene may not experience any problems until the age of twenty or more, although they often have a first heart attack in their thirties or forties.

Heart disease as a result of genetic factors cannot be cured. However, drugs can sometimes be used to help control the disease. Also, the risk can be lessened by adopting healthy eating habits and participating in a program of moderate exercise.

Excess Body Weight

Because people who are overweight are prone to heart disease, losing extra fat can help reduce that risk. Excess weight puts added strain on the heart. In general, the size of the heart is proportional to the normal size of a person's body. If you gain weight, the heart has to work harder than it did when your body was smaller. Obesity also affects the heart by increasing the person's blood pressure and blood cholesterol. Obesity often leads to *diabetes,* and this too increases cholesterol and triglyceride levels in the blood. A person who is 20 percent or more heavier than his or her ideal body weight is usually considered obese.

One important benefit of exercise is that it helps to reduce excess body weight by "burning" excess calories. The calories in the food we eat provide energy for movement and all the body processes. If we consume more calories than our bodies need, they are stored as fat. If we consume fewer calories, the body uses stored fat to provide energy. Calorie needs vary with the individual's size, age, body chemistry, and activity levels. If you are overweight, a combination of an exercise program and a low-calorie diet can help you both to lose weight and strengthen your muscles. Any weight loss program should be done under the supervision of a doctor.

Diabetes

Diabetes is a disease in which the body is unable to properly process sugar. In some cases, diabetes is inherited, but, as mentioned, it may also develop as a result of obesity. Diabetes sharply increases the risk of heart attack because it increases both the cholesterol and triglyceride levels in the blood and also causes damage to blood vessel layers.

Anyone with a family history of diabetes should be aware of possible symptoms of the disease. They include increased thirst, constant hunger, excessive fatigue, or changes in vision. People most likely to develop diabetes are those who are overweight, over forty years old, and related to a diabetic. A doctor can determine whether a person has diabetes with urine and blood tests. Treatments for diabetes include changing eating habits, establishing programs for weight control and exercise, and the use of certain drugs.

Lack of Exercise

According to researchers at the U.S. Center for Disease Control, the nation's most common threat to the heart is physical inactivity. Relatively little exercise, only one hour a day, or enough to burn 200 to 300 calories, is enough to significantly reduce the risk of heart attack. No one knows why moderate exercise is so beneficial. What is known, however, is that exercise helps strengthen heart muscle and reduce cholesterol and blood pressure levels, and may affect other factors in the blood as well.

Exercise helps the heart by lowering the body's level of cholesterol and triglycerides. Exercise promotes the production of HDLs, which remove cholesterol from artery walls, and lowers the levels of LDLs, which stimulate the formation of plaque. Exercise also reduces the level of sugar in the blood and thereby helps to control diabetes, another risk factor for heart disease.

People who exercise regularly and keep themselves in good physical condition are less likely to have heart attacks and, if they do, are usually able to recover from them more easily. Exercise stimulates the heart and promotes the growth of additional coronary blood vessels. These blood vessels not only give the heart an increased blood supply, which helps it to work more efficiently, but also provide secondary routes for blood if one of the main arteries becomes blocked.

A heart that is exercised regularly also becomes stronger so that it works more efficiently while stressed. Normally, the heart responds to sudden exertion by pumping faster, but in someone who has conditioned his or her heart, such as a trained athlete, the ventricles are able to pump more strongly and push out more blood at one time. Thus, even during a race or other physical activity, the person's heart can work longer and stronger to pump the blood that provides the energy needed by the body muscles.

Exercise programs should be developed slowly and carefully, especially by people who have not exercised regularly for a long time. A sudden strain on the heart of a person who has not maintained good physical condition may be dangerous. Too many people suffer heart attacks because they undertake some physical activity such as shoveling snow or playing a strenuous tennis game after months or years of physical inactivity. Such situations can be prevented by developing a sensible program of moderate exercise.

The American Heart Association recommends that adults participate in regular, repetitive exercise. The activity should occur at least three times a week, last thirty minutes or more, and increase the heart rate and

Trained athletes such as short-distance runners demand powerful exertions from their hearts to provide the stamina and energy that their bodies need.

breathing to more than 60 percent of its normal maximum work level. The best exercises for conditioning the heart include jogging, rowing, stationary cycling, swimming, running in place, rope jumping, and cross-country skiing. Exercises such as bicycling, downhill skiing, basketball, calisthenics, handball, racquetball, soccer, squash, tennis (singles), and walking are also good, although they may have to be done longer than thirty minutes to be effective.

The American Heart Association recommends that children be encouraged to participate in physical activities that are appropriate to their age and body development. The ideal is to develop a habit of regular physical activity that the individual will want to maintain throughout life.

Stress

Everyday life in the modern world is filled with stress at many levels, ranging from having to cope with problems like traffic and homework to serious personal crises such as divorce and death. One of the natural responses to a stressful situation is that the body produces more adrenaline. If a person is constantly stressed, the increased level of adrenaline in the blood can put a strain on the heart by interfering with the normal actions of cholesterol. The adrenaline may also speed the buildup of plaque in the arteries.

Often it is possible to eliminate some of the causes of stress or to learn to overcome reactions which lead to feelings of tension. Exercise can also be useful for reducing the tensions of everyday life.

Drugs

In the summer of 1986, a star college athlete, Len Bias, died of a cocaine overdose. The actual cause of death, however, was a heart attack, initiated by the action of the powerful drug.

As cocaine enters the body, it travels in the bloodstream to the brain, where it stimulates the production of adrenaline. At the same time, the drug blocks the body's normal ability to reabsorb adrenaline. This results in a huge surge of adrenaline to the heart. Cocaine can also disrupt the brain's ability to send signals to the heart. In either case, a heart attack can result.

Cocaine is an extremely dangerous drug. Unlike some other drugs, users do not build up a tolerance for it, so that the same dose used one day can be fatal the next, particularly if its purity is unknown. Unfortunately, the use of cocaine is rising among young people. The lesson of tragic deaths like that of Len Bias is that drugs like cocaine are deadly and should be avoided at all cost.

Smoking

Every package of cigarettes sold in the United States bears this message: "SURGEON GENERAL'S WARNING: Smoking By Pregnant Women May Result in Fetal Injury, Premature Birth, And Low Birth Weight." Studies have also shown that a person who smokes is twice as likely to have a heart attack than someone who does not smoke and is two to four times

In 1986, basketball star Len Bias (with ball) died of a heart attack as a result of a cocaine overdose.

as likely to die from the heart attack. Contrary to what most people believe, the biggest danger of smoking is not lung disease, but heart attacks and coronary artery disease. It is estimated that 30 percent of all coronary heart disease deaths each year result from smoking.

Smoking affects the heart in several ways. Regular smoking lowers the level of HDL compounds, which normally help rid the body of excess cholesterol. Smoking also promotes the development of atherosclerosis, increases blood pressure, and decreases the amount of oxygen available to the heart.

Even smoking just a few cigarettes a day brings the risk of heart disease; smoking a pack or more a day can increase the risk of heart disease to more than five times that of a nonsmoker. Nonsmokers who are constantly exposed to cigarette smoke in the air may also increase their risk of heart disease. For instance, in a recent study, it was shown that adolescent boys who lived in homes with smokers had levels of HDLs in their blood 10 percent lower than boys who lived with nonsmokers. The reduced HDL levels could lead to a buildup of cholesterol in their bodies.

The good news is that people who stop smoking can almost completely reduce their level of risk to that of people who never smoked. Public education programs in recent years have helped to reduce the number of people who smoke; yet smoking remains the leading avoidable cause of heart disease. As the American Heart Association says, "It's important to stop smoking before the signs of heart disease appear, so if you don't smoke, don't start. And if you do smoke, quit. STOP SMOKING NOW!"

CHAPTER

8

DIAGNOSING AND TREATING HEART DISEASE

A hundred years ago, there was almost no treatment for heart disease. If your heart was weak, you simply suffered and died. Today, a wide variety of techniques have been developed to diagnose heart disease. Once the problem has been analyzed, the physician can choose a course of treatment which may vary, from the use of drugs and nonsurgical techniques to open heart surgery.

Diagnosis

Like the other internal organs, the heart can be seen and examined directly only during surgery. To understand how the heart functions, physicians must rely on information that is gained by listening to it or "looking" at it with the help of X rays, computers, or other devices.

An *electrocardiogram (ECG or EKG)* is one of the basic tools used to find out how well the heart is working. Small sensors placed on the chest are used to measure the amount of electrical activity around the heart during each beat. This appears as a rhythmic rise and fall on the ECG screen. Sometimes the ECG is taken while the patient is running on a treadmill or riding a stationary bicycle. If part of the ECG wave becomes depressed, it means that not enough blood is reaching the heart muscle, and this effect is magnified when the heart is stressed. Changes in the tracing of the ECG can reveal where there might be damaged or healing tissue and provide evidence that a person has had a heart attack even when there may not have been any pain.

In a technique called *cardiac catheterization,* a thin hollow tube is inserted into a blood vessel of the arm or leg. The tube, called a catheter, is then pushed carefully through the blood vessel system until it reaches the heart. There, the heart's pressure can be measured and blood samples can be taken. If the catheter is used to inject dye into the heart, an X ray can help show the pattern of blood flow.

Angiocardiography is a technique in which dye is injected into the heart and circulatory system and photographed with X-ray motion pictures or with videotapes. These can then be replayed to allow the physician to analyze the problem in detail. In a variation of the angiocardiography technique, known as digital cardiac angiography, the action of the heart and blood vessels is recorded by computer.

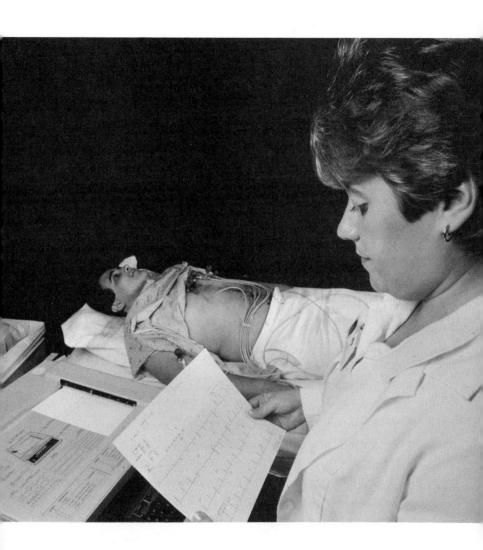

The ECG wave in an electrocardiogram test may reveal where heart damage has occurred. It may even show that a person has had a heart attack even when the patient has not suffered any pain.

Echocardiography provides a picture of the heart through the use of high-frequency ultrasound waves. In this painless procedure, the ultrasound waves penetrate the chest. As they bounce off the heart, they can reveal extremely small details in its structure. They can also be used to look at the larger blood vessels.

Radionuclide imaging involves injecting mildly radioactive substances into the bloodstream and following them with the help of computers. The computer produces a picture which shows how well the heart muscle is supplied with blood and how well the heart is working. This technique can also be used to determine which part of the heart has been damaged in a heart attack.

A *CAT scanner* is a large X-ray machine that moves along part of the body taking a continuous X ray. A computer can then select any portion, or slice, of the three-dimensional picture to show what is happening at a specific location. Although CAT scanners are sometimes used to look at hearts, physicians prefer to avoid the use of X rays whenever possible because they are potentially dangerous.

A new, safer technique called *magnetic resonance imaging* (sometimes called *MRI* or *NMR*) uses strong magnets rather than X rays to ''see'' inside the body and provides the same kind of information as a CAT scanner. Computers use the information for several purposes: to make pictures of heart muscle, to show damage from a heart attack, to diagnose certain kinds of congenital defects, or to look at some of the larger blood vessels.

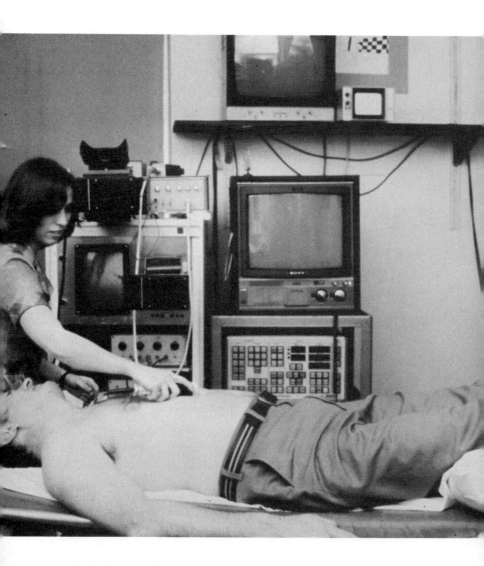

Echocardiography is a painless procedure wherein ultrasound waves penetrate the chest and bounce off the heart, recording intricate details about its structure.

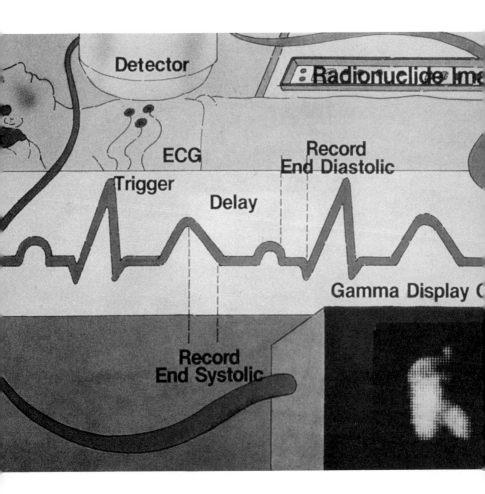

This diagram shows how the radionuclide imaging technique can generate a computer picture showing the heart's performance.

Drugs That Combat
Heart Disease

One of the recent breakthroughs in the study of heart disease was the discovery that people who take one aspirin every other day are less likely to have a first heart attack than those who do not take aspirin regularly. Scientists have known for a long time that aspirin, which is usually used to suppress pain, also impairs the clotting of blood by preventing the production of a family of hormones called *prostaglandins*. Prostaglandins aid clotting by making blood platelets sticky. Most heart attacks are the result of a clot blocking a blood vessel that supplies the heart, and aspirin helps prevent such clots from forming. Studies have now shown that aspirin not only reduces the risk of a first heart attack, it also lowers the risk of a second heart attack for those who have already had one. The other commonly used painkillers, acetaminophen and ibuprofen, do not prevent heart attacks.

The use of aspirin to prevent heart attacks should be done only under a doctor's supervision. In some people, aspirin can cause nausea, internal bleeding, or an allergic reaction. Aspirin should not be given to chidren with viral infections because it may cause Reye's syndrome, a rare and sometimes fatal childhood disease.

Aspirin is among a group of drugs called *anticoagulants*. They are often used to treat heart disease because they prevent clots from forming and dissolve clots that already exist. Anticoagulants must be used carefully because a dose that is too high could cause a patient to bleed to death from a minor injury.

Vasodilators, drugs that dilate, or widen, the arteries, are often used to treat heart disease. The most commonly used vasodilator is nitroglycerin, a drug that relaxes blood vessels, allowing the heart to work less hard; at the same time, it increases the heart's blood supply by expanding the coronary arteries. As the blood flow to the heart improves, more oxygen reaches the heart and it works more efficiently.

Another group of drugs, called *beta blockers,* help prevent heart attacks by blocking the effects of adrenaline and a related hormone, noradrenaline. Normally, these hormones stimulate the heart to beat stronger and faster and help to raise the blood pressure. For people who have heart disease, stress on the heart can be dangerous, so by interfering with this process, the beta blockers help protect the heart.

Calcium channel blockers affect the muscle contractions of the heart. Normally, calcium is needed for muscle cells to contract, and if there is not enough calcium available, the muscles contract less forcefully. Calcium channel blockers can help reduce the pressure and force of the heart and allow it to "rest." They also help lower blood pressure by reducing the strength of the rhythmic contractions of the arteries.

Physicians sometimes prescribe anticholesterol drugs to help lower the level of LDLs in the bloodstream when other efforts to reduce blood cholesterol fail. Some of these drugs help remove LDLs from the blood, while others block an enzyme that the liver needs to manufacture cholesterol. Because most of the anticholesterol drugs have unpleasant or possibly dangerous side effects, they are used only when absolutely necessary.

Nonsurgical Remedies
for Heart Disease

Several nonsurgical techniques are available to help widen or clean out clogged arteries so that blood flow can increase. One of these, *angioplasty,* consists of inserting a flexible hollow tube called a catheter into an artery of the arm or leg and carefully threading it through the arteries until it reaches the location of an obstruction. Then a smaller, balloon-tipped catheter is inserted into the first one and pushed until the tip emerges from the open end of the larger catheter near the plaque. The balloon is then inflated, and its pressure compresses the plaque against the artery wall, thus allowing blood to flow more freely. The balloon is then deflated and both catheters are removed.

A new technique for cleaning out plaque-filled arteries uses a catheter with a laser tip. The laser's beam of highly concentrated light removes the plaque from the artery wall. This technique has been used only on the large arteries of the leg, but as finer, more accurate laser tubes are developed, it will be used to clean coronary and other arteries as well.

Another new method works like a tiny Roto-Rooter inside the arteries. A small catheter with a rotating blade at its tip is inserted into a clogged artery, and the blades are used to cut away the plaque. Currently, the technique is being used only on large arteries in the legs but, like the laser, will soon be available to clean out arteries of the heart.

Heart Surgery

As a remedy, surgery is the last option, and is used only when drugs and nonsurgical techniques do not offer sufficient help to a failing heart.

The Heart-Lung Machine

Heart surgery was rarely attempted before the development of the heart-lung machine. For any kind of surgical procedure in or near the heart, the heart's action must be temporarily stopped. However, if the body tissues have their oxygen supply cut off, they will quickly die. The role of the heart-lung machine is to supply the body with oxygenated blood until the surgical procedure is over and the heartbeat resumes.

The heart-lung machine collects blood from the veins and stores it in a compartment from which it flows into the oxygenator. In the body, blood normally picks up oxygen as it passes through the lungs. There, 300 million tiny air sacs providing a surface area of 84 square yards (70 sqm), are the meeting place for blood and air. The heart-lung machine imitates this process by bubbling oxygen through the blood. At the same time, carbon dioxide is removed from the blood and the blood temperature is monitored. The blood then flows into a chamber which removes any bubbles, and from there it flows back into the body. The heart-lung machine can keep the patient's body alive for hours and allows surgeons to

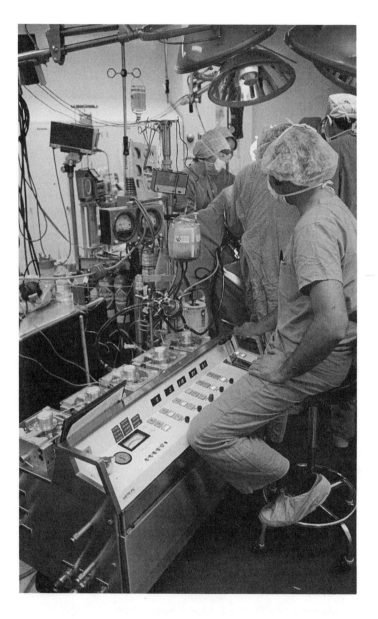

The heart-lung machine supplies the body with oxygenated blood during open-heart surgery.

perform lengthy and complicated operations on the heart.

Surgical Procedures

If one of the blood vessels leading to the heart becomes hopelessly clogged, then it must be replaced. In this procedure, called coronary artery bypass graft surgery, surgeons take a large blood vessel from another part of the body, usually from the leg or inside the chest wall, and use it to make a detour around the blocked section of the coronary artery. They attach one end of the new blood vessel above the blockage and the other below it, thus allowing the blood to flow around the blockage.

A much more radical procedure is the heart transplant, in which the diseased heart is almost completely removed and replaced with a healthy heart. When the first heart transplant was performed in 1967 by South African surgeon Dr. Christiaan Barnard, it was headline news. Since then there have been more than 10,000 heart transplant operations worldwide, and nearly 6,000 of the patients who received those hearts are still alive. The first transplant recipient, Louis Washkansky, lived only eighteen days, but now, on average, more than 80 percent of the recipients live for one year and more than 75 percent survive more than five years.

Transplant recipients are usually patients whose hearts are so weak or damaged that they will die within six months without a replacement. These people must wait until a donor heart becomes available. Usually the donor heart comes from an accident victim whose

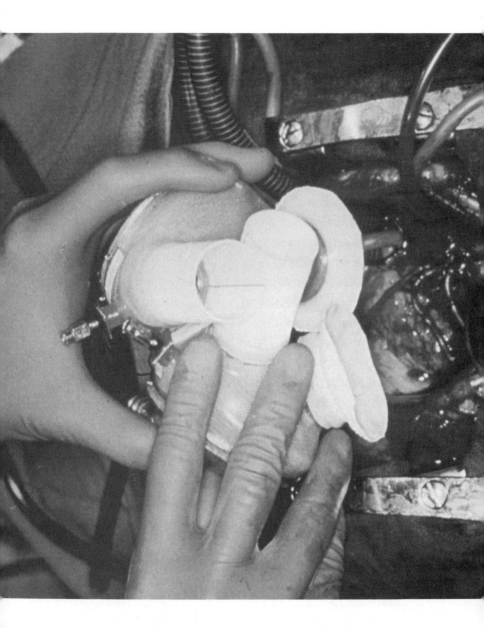

*An artificial heart is carefully implanted
in a patient's chest.*

brain has been irreparably injured but whose heart still functions normally.

Early heart transplants were complicated by the body's tendency to reject the heart as foreign tissue just as it would reject invading bacteria. Today, that problem has been mostly solved with the use of a drug called cyclosporin A which destroys the white corpuscles, or white blood cells, which are part of the body's immune system. If not destroyed, the white blood cells would identify the substances in the new heart as foreign and would attack them, eventually destroying the heart.

One of the problems with heart transplants as a solution to heart disease is the limited number of available hearts. Not everyone who needs a new heart is able to get one. One alternative is to use an artificial heart. The first artificial heart was used in 1981 to temporarily replace the failing heart of a man until a donor heart could be located. The following year, an artificial heart was used for the first time as a permanent replacement for a diseased heart. The mechanical heart, called the Jarvik-7 after the man who invented it, was implanted in Barney Clark, a retired dentist in Utah. Barney Clark lived for 118 days.

Artificial hearts are most often used to keep seriously ill patients alive while they are waiting for a donor heart. Artificial hearts are a potentially valuable weapon in the battle against heart disease. However, until all the problems of the artificial heart are solved the living heart is still the most efficient device known for keeping the body supplied with the blood it needs.

CHAPTER

9

THE FUTURE

Will we conquer heart disease in the near future? Probably not. Predictions by U.S. government agencies say that despite changes in life-style and new medical treatments, it will still be the number one cause of death well into the twenty-first century. Nevertheless, many recent advances in the battle against heart disease are providing hope for heart disease patients.

Medical researchers are finding ways in which heart disease can be controlled through the use of devices such as artificial pacemakers, new forms of surgery, and the development of life-saving drugs. One of the most interesting new devices for heart patients is the Nimbus Hemopump, a tiny pump that helps circulate blood through the body. The pump, which is about a centimeter (0.4 inch) long, is inserted into the heart through a catheter in the leg. It works like a miniature fan pulling blood out of the left ventricle and into the aorta. Although the pump is still in an experimental stage, it is believed that it has the potential to save more than 100,000 lives each year.

Basic research into how the heart and circulatory system work also has led to discoveries that can help victims of heart disease. For instance, scientists studying beavers and other mammals that stay underwater for long periods have learned that when one of these animals dives into the water, a reaction takes place which causes changes in the circulatory system. The heartbeat slows down, which reduces its own need for oxygen, and more blood is routed to organs, such as the brain, that are easily damaged by lack of oxygen. Doctors have used this information to treat patients with one kind of abnormally fast heartbeat. The face of the patient is briefly immersed in chilly water, and the same kind of reflex triggers a slower, more normal rhythm.

Studies of bears may lead us to a better knowledge of how cholesterol is used in the body. In the months before its annual winter hibernation, a bear develops huge fat reserves. This fat provides the energy the bear's body needs during the long months when it does not eat. Although the bears have extremely high levels of cholesterol, they do not deposit plaque on their artery walls as many people with high cholesterol levels do. As we learn how bears avoid atherosclerosis, the knowledge may help us find new treatments for people with this problem.

As we have become more aware of foods that contribute to heart disease, the food industry has responded by making healthier foods available. We can now buy more low-fat and low-salt foods in the market. In restaurants and on airlines, there are often special diets for people who need to reduce their cholesterol or sodium intake. School lunch programs now also reflect more awareness of the need to keep fatty foods at a minimum.

Exercise programs have also become increasingly popular, and more people are now trying to keep their bodies fit. Special programs for all ages, from infants to the elderly, help people find the right kinds of activities for their age and physical condition. It is important to develop the habit of exercise early, particularly in a world that is becoming increasingly sedentary.

Another important weapon in the battle against heart disease is public education. Many school systems have created programs to educate both students and parents about the need for changing dietary habits and getting more exercise. In some communities, free or low-cost cholesterol screening is also available. Some health education programs, particularly for junior high school–age students, focus on the prevention of cigarette smoking to avoid heart disease. Because many of the factors that lead to heart disease—life-style, exercise, dietary habits, and smoking—are developed early in life, the American Heart Association has produced for preschool children a kit called the Heart Treasure Chest. The kit includes activities, songs, and games that help young children learn about the heart and encourage the development of healthy habits.

Heart disease is still with us, but as we learn to

recognize its causes and symptoms, we will, in many cases, be able to control its effect on our lives. The future for victims of heart disease is brighter today than it has ever been before, but, as always, the best cure for this number one killer is to prevent its development whenever possible.

GLOSSARY

adrenaline: a hormone that speeds up the heartbeat. It is produced by the adrenal glands; also called epinephrine.

aldosterone: a substance that causes the kidneys to retain sodium. It is produced by the adrenal glands.

angina pectoris: severe chest pains caused by a lack of blood supply to heart muscles. Also called angina.

angiocardiography: the use of dye and X rays to observe how the heart is working.

angioplasty: a technique used to open clogged arteries.

anticoagulants: drugs that prevent clotting.

antihypertensives: drugs that lower blood pressure.

aorta: the largest artery in the body; receives oxygenated blood pumped from the left ventricle of the heart.

arrythmia: any kind of abnormal rhythm in the heartbeat.

arteries: vessels that carry blood away from the heart. They have thick muscular walls to withstand the pressure of the blood.

arteriole: a narrow artery which can become wider or narrower as necessary to regulate the blood flow.

arteriosclerosis: the general term for the thickening and hardening of the arteries.

atherosclerosis: a buildup of plaque on the inner lining of the arteries.

atrioventricular node: the structure in the heart which relays electric impulses from the atria to the ventricles.

atrioventricular valves: openings between the atria and ventricles covered by flaps of tissue that open and close to permit blood to flow only in one direction.

atrium or auricle: either of the two chambers in the upper part of the heart which receive blood from the body or lungs. The plural of "atrium" is "atria".

auricle: see atrium.

autonomic nerves: nerves that automatically control basic body functions, including the heartbeat.

bacterial endocarditis: a bacterial infection of the heart valves or tissues lining the heart.

beta blockers: drugs that block certain hormones that stimulate the heart.

bicuspid valve or mitral valve: the valve between the atrium and ventricle on the left side of the heart.

blood pressure: the measure of pressure on the walls of the blood vessels; correlated with the amount of pressure used by the heart to pump blood through the body.

bradycardia: a heart rate that is too slow.

calcium channel blockers: drugs that affect muscle contractions of the heart.

capillaries: the smallest blood vessels in the body. Oxygen and carbon dioxide pass in and out of the blood through the thin walls of the capillaries.

cardiac catheterization: a diagnostic procedure involving the insertion of a tube through the blood vessels to the heart.

cardiac veins: vessels which carry deoxygenated blood away from the heart.

cardiopulmonary resuscitation (CPR): emergency treatment for heart attack victims.

CAT scanner: a machine used to take a continuous X ray of part of the body.

catheter: a narrow tube that can be inserted into a blood vessel or other body duct.

cerebral embolism: a stroke caused by a clot brought to the brain from elsewhere in the body.

cerebral thrombosis: a stroke caused by a blood clot formed in an artery leading to the brain.

cholesterol: a yellowish fatty substance found in the blood.

clot or thrombus: a clump of blood cells. Clots are produced by a chemical reaction between blood factors and platelets. Also called a thrombus.

coronary arteries: vessels which supply oxygenated blood to the heart.

coronary occlusion: see coronary thrombosis.

coronary thrombosis or coronary occlusion: a kind of heart attack.

CPR: see cardiopulmonary resuscitation.

cyanosis: a condition caused by poorly oxygenated blood. Cyanosis makes the skin appear blue in the lips and around the fingernails.

defibrillator: a device which shocks the heart to stimulate normal beating.

diabetes: a disorder in which the body is unable to process sugar normally.

diastole: the part of the heartbeat when the heart is relaxing; the second number given in a blood pressure reading.

diuretics: drugs that rid the body of excess salts and water.

ductus arteriosus: the blood vessel in an infant that links the aorta and pulmonary artery and thereby enables the blood to bypass the lungs.

echocardiography: the use of ultrasound waves to look at the heart.

electrocardiogram (ECG or EKG): the tracing of electric impulses produced by the heart as it beats.

fibrillation: an uncontrolled quivering of the heart muscle.

fibrin: tiny yellow fibers that produce a clot to block a wound. Fibrin is produced by platelets from substances dissolved in the blood.

HDL: high-density lipoproteins; remove cholesterol from artery walls and prevent its deposit there.

heart attack: see myocardial infarction.

hemiplegia: a paralysis of either the right or left half of the body as a result of a stroke.

hemoglobin: substance found in red blood cells that contains iron. It combines easily with oxygen and carries it to body cells.

hypercholesterolemia: a high level of cholesterol in the blood.

hypertension: the medical term for high blood pressure.

(103)

inferior vena cava: the large vessel which returns deoxygenated blood from the lower body to the heart.

ischemia: the suppression of blood flow.

Kawasaki disease: a childhood disease which sometimes causes temporary damage to the heart.

LDL: low-density lipoproteins; bring cholesterol from the liver to the body cells.

lipoproteins: substances which transport cholesterol and other lipids in the body.

magnetic resonance imaging (MRI or NMR): the use of strong magnets to look inside the body.

mitral valve: see bicuspid valve.

MRI: see magnetic resonance imaging.

myocardial infarction or heart attack: the death of heart tissue that results from a reduction or complete stoppage of the blood supply to the heart.

myocardial ischemia: the reduction of blood flow to the heart.

myocardium: heart tissue.

NMR: see magnetic resonance imaging.

pacemaker, or sinus node: the area in the right atrium which produces electrical impulses that cause the heart to beat regularly. If the natural pacemaker fails, an electronic pacemaker can be fitted surgically.

pericarditis: an inflammation of the pericardium.

pericardium: the outer wrapping of the heart. Fluid between the heart and the pericardium lubricates the heart as it pumps.

placenta: an organ developed in the uterus during pregnancy that nourishes the fetus (unborn baby).

plaque: the buildup of fats, cholesterol, waste products, and calcium on the blood vessel walls.

plasma: the clear liquid in which red and white blood cells and platelets are suspended. Plasma contains many food materials needed by the body as well as dissolved wastes.

platelets: small pieces of cells floating in the blood which take part in the production of blood clots and help close wounds.

prostaglandins: a group of hormones that aid clotting by making blood platelets sticky.

pulmonary artery: the vessel that carries deoxygenated blood from the heart to the lungs.

pulmonary veins: the vessels that return oxygenated blood from the lungs to the heart.

radionuclide imaging: the use of radioactive substances to look at the heart.

red blood cells: see red corpuscles.

red corpuscles, or red blood cells: cells in the blood that contain hemoglobin and transport oxygen to the body cells.

renin: a substance produced by the kidneys which causes blood vessels to contract.

rheumatic fever: a disease which can cause permanent damage to the heart.

semilunar valves: valves at the openings between the ventricles and the aorta and pulmonary artery.

septum: the strong wall dividing the left and right sides of the heart.

sinus node: see pacemaker.

sphygmomanometer: an instrument used to measure blood pressure.

stethoscope: an instrument with which sounds such as the heartbeat can be heard inside the body.

Streptococcus: a bacterium that causes strep throat, rheumatic fever, scarlet fever, and other illnesses.

superior vena cava: the large vessel that returns deoxygenated blood from the upper body to the heart.

systole: the part of the heartbeat when the heart is contracting; the first number given in a blood pressure reading.

tachycardia: a heart rate that is too fast.

thrombus: see clot.

transient ischemic attack (TIA): a ministroke that occurs when a blood vessel in the brain is temporarily blocked.

tricuspid valve: opening between the atrium and ventricle on the right side of the heart.

triglycerides: fatty substances in the blood that contribute to heart disease.

vasodilators: drugs that expand blood vessels.

veins: thin-walled blood vessels which return blood to the heart.

ventricle: one of the two lower chambers of the heart which pump blood either to the lungs or around the body.

venules: the smallest veins.

white blood cells: see white corpuscles.

white corpuscles, or white blood cells: cells in the blood that combat harmful bacteria in the body.

FOR FURTHER READING

Berger, Melvin. *The Artificial Heart*. New York: Franklin Watts, 1987.

Facklam, Margery, and Howard Facklam. New York: *Spare Parts for People*. Harcourt, Brace, Jovanovich, 1987.

Limburg, Peter. *The Story of Your Heart*. New York: Coward, McCann and Geoghegan, 1979.

Madison, Arnold. *Transplanted and Artificial Body Organs*. New York: Beaufort Books, 1981.

Silverstein, Dr. Alvin, and Virginia B. Silverstein. *Heart Disease: America's #1 Killer*. Philadelphia: J. B. Lippincott, 1976, 1985.

Ward, Brian R. *The Heart and Blood*. New York: Franklin Watts, 1982.

You can also obtain valuable information about heart disease either by contacting The American Heart Association in your own city or by writing to The American Heart Association, National Center, 7320 Greenville Avenue, Dallas, TX 75231.

INDEX

(109)